TH
HAPPY
TANK

PRAISE FOR
THE HAPPY TANK

PUPILS' FEEDBACK

Briony - Year 6

In the morning when I practise filling my Happy Tank if I am ever feeling sad, I know that two minutes on each level of *The Happy Tank* can make me feel happier. I have noticed other Kind Kids see how happy and confident I am.

Johnny - Year 6

I like *The Happy Tank* because when I wake up early it gets me ready for the day and I have noticed when I get to school, I pay more attention to the teacher and I feel relaxed and calm.

Abi - Year 9

Since practising the exercises in *The Happy Tank* in the morning, I feel less upset and depressed, happier and more self-confident. The book has helped my mental health. I also have more friends now because I am happier in myself. It really does work, you just have to do what it says, which is easy peasy lemon squeezy, and to practise, practise, practise.

Tori - Year 9

What I have learnt from practising the exercises in *The Happy Tank* is to not take life too seriously and to have fun whilst learning new things. It has shown me that we can always make time to take care of our own wellbeing.

Scott - Year 6

The Happy Tank will help other pupils because it makes you think happier thoughts. It helps me reflect on my choices and I believe it will help other children too.

Mackenzie - Year 6

It can help other children by helping them calm down and not be as angry or sad. It keeps them in a good state of mind. I like the way it helps me calm down.

Sophie - Year 6

It helped me with my anger, I tend to get angry very easily and it has helped me calm down and not have as many behaviour incidents inside and outside of the classroom. I would say if you have a short temper, practise the exercises in *The Happy Tank* and it will help you have less anger.

Zara - Year 6

It has made me feel happier throughout the day. I used to get moody a lot throughout the day, but now I don't as much. I think it can help other children feel calmer.

BLOOMSBURY EDUCATION
Bloomsbury Publishing Plc
50 Bedford Square, London, WC1B 3DP, UK
29 Earlsfort Terrace, Dublin 2, Ireland

BLOOMSBURY, BLOOMSBURY EDUCATION and the Diana logo
are trademarks of Bloomsbury Publishing Plc

First published in Great Britain, 2023

ISBN: PB: 978-1-8019-9231-2; ePDF: 978-1-8019-9233-6; ePub: 978-1-8019-9232-9

2 4 6 8 10 9 7 5 3 (paperback)

Interior design by Jeni Child

Printed and bound in the UK by CPI Group (UK) Ltd, Croydon, CR0 4YY

To find out more about our authors and books visit www.bloomsbury.com
and sign up for our newsletters

THE HAPPY TANK

Fill your life with happy habits

JOHN MAGEE

BLOOMSBURY EDUCATION

LONDON   OXFORD   NEW YORK   NEW DELHI   SYDNEY

This book is dedicated to Chris Lickiss, National Leader of Education and Executive Headteacher, the kindest gentleman I have ever met, who taught me so much about the importance of valuing others and how to create amazing relationships.

Thank you Chris for helping me transform so many children's lives.

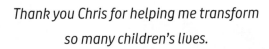

CONTENTS

FOREWORD

What an honour it is to write a foreword for this book! Its central topic of happiness is very dear to my heart. When I was at primary school, I used to think about it a great deal. Why are some happy and others not? Why do my feelings of happiness seem to fade – like the ever-dimming memory of a holiday and lingering feeling of sadness at its distant recollection. I think many of us grow up thinking about questions like these as we try to understand life and what it entails.

Many thinkers such as the ancient Greek philosopher, Aristotle, and Tibetan spiritual leader, the Dalai Lama (whom you will catch a glimpse of later on in this book) held the belief that happiness is our ultimate goal in life – in other words, that it is not a constant state but something to be strived for in our actions and the relationships we foster around us and in the type of lifestyle we choose and can feel a sense of pride in.

Both Aristotle and the Dalai Lama believed that leading a happier life ultimately derives from our habits and day-to-day actions. "We are what we repeatedly do," Aristotle once wrote. "Happiness is not something ready-made, it comes from our own actions," the Dalai Lama said. Learning to be happier comes from the actions we carry out on a *daily* basis.

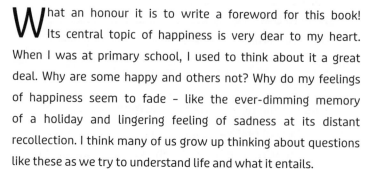

This is precisely where this book comes into the picture! Its author, John Magee, is a 21st century Aristotle, with the wisdom of the Dalai Lama, and the looks and humour of Paddy McGuinness (if unknown to you, look him up – the resemblance is to all accounts uncanny)! His book, *The Happy Tank*, is a practical guide on how to forego old, unhelpful habits and start new ones afresh that help us to feel happier for longer. You will learn how to take care of yourself better; how to use your breath to stay calm; how to reflect on what you want in life; how to be kinder; how to use affirmations to talk to yourself in a more supportive way; how to be grateful for what you have; and finally how to happy tap (I invite you to read on and find out about that!).

What I also love about this book is that John Magee shows us how to accept, even embrace our more uncomfortable emotions like sadness, anger or jealousy. As John says, feelings each have their place and none will ever stick around forever. A key to happiness is learning how to be okay no matter what the feeling we experience!

I hope you enjoy reading this book as much as I have and choose to embark on The Happy Tank Challenge to see how it can make a difference to your life and that of those you love – sharing is caring.

ADRIAN BETHUNE

Author of *Wellbeing in the Primary Classroom*.

Please sign your online pledge today to bring about change in your life and the lives of other pupils by visiting **www.kindnessmatters.co.uk/thehappytank**.

Visit my YouTube channel Kindness Matters TV and search The Happy Tank Challenge to take your practice to another level. Perhaps you will teach a grown-up, family member or friend. If you want more help in improving your daily practice, the video content is a great way to do so.

You will become part of a whole community of Kind Kids who like to take care of their mental health and wellbeing and learn new ways to feel calm and relaxed, which is important, is it not? Enjoy the book, have fun and never take yourself too seriously, while learning and getting better at creating happy habits by filling your Happy Tank daily... NOW, let's *pass it on!*

THIS BOOK BELONGS TO

....

**I pledge to complete my
Happy Tank Challenge from this book.**

**I will then teach one or more parts
of what I have learnt from
The Happy Tank to a handful of
my friends or family members,
on the condition they pledge
to pass it on and do the same!**

Dated...

HOW TO USE THIS BOOK IF YOU ARE A PUPIL

- Set aside 10 to 20 minutes to learn from each exercise.

- Read a section from *The Happy Tank* and practise its corresponding exercise first thing in the morning.

- Follow the book and work your way through the exercises at your own pace, aiming to become a master of each one. It doesn't matter how long you take to complete the book, you just need to stick at it and have fun! Remember practice makes progress, so go easy on yourself as you begin to create daily happy habits.

- Practise in the evening just before bed to support a deep relaxing sleep.

- If you feel worried or overwhelmed by things in life, practise filling your Happy Tank by choosing an exercise to complete.

- Make a daily commitment to yourself to fill your Happy Tank; this will create positivity to form happy habits.

You might use this book if you are...

- Afraid about your SATs.

- Worried about moving up a year group.

- Worried about transitioning into secondary school.

- Having a lot of thoughts running around your head.

- Wanting to learn new ways to calm down and worry less.

- Having unhelpful thoughts.

HOW TO USE THIS BOOK IF YOU ARE A TEACHER

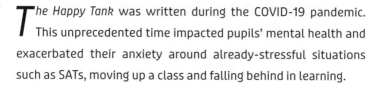

*T*he *Happy Tank* was written during the COVID-19 pandemic. This unprecedented time impacted pupils' mental health and exacerbated their anxiety around already-stressful situations such as SATs, moving up a class and falling behind in learning.

In this challenging context, I joined KS2 pupils in a year 6 setting at Westminster Primary Academy in Blackpool to develop an e-learning programme with six exercises to practise at school and at home to help reduce and manage unhelpful emotions.

All pupils responded exceptionally well to carrying out the exercises in their daily routine. They practised one exercise in the book each morning for a week as a collective at school, then again before bed with a parent or carer (and in time alone), before moving on to another exercise the following week and so on. The programme gave birth to *The Happy Tank* book that you hold in your hand now. Even though the book was written with a year 6 group, the book can still work well with KS3 pupils.

Here are some ways you can support your pupils' mental health and wellbeing.

- After registering your pupils, start the morning by reading a section of *The Happy Tank* to them, and applying its corresponding exercise. You can ask pupils to read along with you using their individual copy of the book.

- Make sure you follow the book sequentially and build up the exercises, moving up from breath work, to reflection and so on and so forth. At the end of the book, pupils should be well versed and will have practised each daily exercise with their peers and teacher.

- Practise individual sections and exercises in your whole-school assemblies. This is an excellent way for your school to collaborate as a whole and support your cohort's mental health and wellbeing.

- After lunch, it can be challenging for pupils to balance their energy. Build in protected time for pupils to fill one or more parts of their Happy Tank to help them to feel calm, relaxed and ready to learn.

- At the end of the school day, make time to review the section and exercise that your pupils have completed that day. This will allow them to reflect on the day itself as well as setting them up for their evening and the following morning.

HOW TO USE THIS BOOK IF YOU ARE A PARENT OR CARER

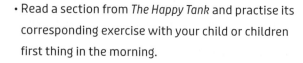

Personally, as a parent, my children love to spend time with me filling their Happy Tank, and I truly enjoy the experience of sharing quiet time with them to do this whilst creating lifelong memories. It is a joy for me to see this being replicated by my pupils and their families in their respective home settings. Here are some ways you can support your child in filling their Happy Tank.

- Read a section from *The Happy Tank* and practise its corresponding exercise with your child or children first thing in the morning.

- Set aside 10 to 20 minutes after reading a chapter to discuss what you and your child have both learned and the experience you had doing its corresponding exercise together.

- Help your child or children use the book sequentially and build up exercises – spend as much time as you need on each exercise and only move on once it has been fully mastered.

- Practise the exercises before doing homework with your children to help them focus their attention.

- Practise with your children in the evening just before bed to support a deep relaxing sleep.

- If your child feels worried or overwhelmed by things in life, practise filling your Happy Tanks together.

- Make a daily commitment to yourself and your children to fill your Happy Tanks; this will create positivity and form happy habits.

INTRODUCTION TO
THE HAPPY TANK

What if there was a way to be happier in life and less sad? Wouldn't you like that? Let me be honest, it is impossible to be happy all of the time. Can you imagine always walking around with a big smile on your face and never experiencing other feelings? There would be no fun in that. In fact, that would be boring!

But if you are like me and all the pupils I work with in schools, who like to be referred to as Kind Kids, I imagine you would like to be happier (even if you're not happy all the time).

If that is the case, you are in the right place and are going to be amazed when you find out how easy peasy lemon squeezy it is to increase your levels of happiness.

It is simple – you have to accept that every day you will go through lots of feelings, including sadness, worry, anger, loneliness and many more upsetting emotions. Doesn't sound too happy, does it? Just trust me and keep reading.

Amidst all these feelings, did you know happiness is a choice? *What do you mean, a choice?* I hear you ask. Well, it just is! And I can swear that on my cat's life! I am going to teach you how you can be happier without having to swear on your cat's life, or if you don't have a cat, your dog's life, guinea pig's life, rabbit's life or goldfish's life. Okay, enough with the pet talk, I think you get my point.

Would you like to know another well-hidden truth I share with my family, friends and thousands of other Kind Kids like you? Being happier is easy; it is a daily practice, and one I will teach in this book. I will use a little humour because all the Kind Kids I have had the pleasure to work with tell me it puts a smile on their faces and makes them laugh, and if you didn't know, now you know: laughing is good for your mental health and wellbeing.

Back to my original point – *The Happy Tank* has changed many Kind Kids' lives and now, it will also change yours. You are your Happy Tank and by learning mindfulness-based exercises, practising them daily and creating happy habits, the exercises will fill your Happy Tank (which is you) and bring an abundance of happiness and calmness to your life.

NOW PAUSE FOR A MINUTE!

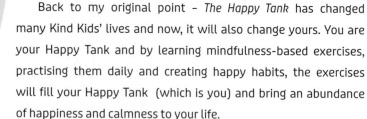

Close the book and look at the front cover... What can you read under the title? 'Fill your life with happy habits'. Remember, happiness is a choice. Has it ever occurred to you that, by choosing to make a few simple changes, your life could change for the better, forever? I can just imagine the smile on your face when reading these words. The few small choices you make every day can bring about a HUGE amount of happiness in your life, in fact, more happiness than you can shake a stick at.

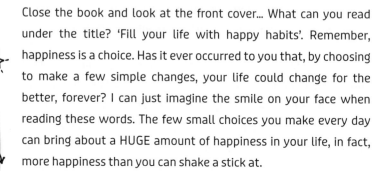

That was meant as an analogy, and if you don't know what that means, then ask your amazing teacher or a grown up. Remember, every day is a chance to learn something new and if you don't understand something, ask a question and get an answer to it!

WARNING!

Turning the next page will begin your journey of having more daily happiness in your life. Hold onto your cap, and if you don't have a cap, grip the book tight, because you are about to start on the journey of a lifetime. Before you flip the page, answer the questions below:

- **It is important to do things that make you feel happy, is it not?**
- **You are interested in feeling happier more of the time, are you not?**
- **It is good to learn new ways to be happier more of the time, is it not?**

EVERY DAY IS A CHANCE TO LEARN SOMETHING NEW

MY STORY

H i, my name is John Magee, the Kindness Coach. I imagine you know what kindness means, but what on earth is a kindness coach? Well, here are some easy peasy lemon squeezy clues:

- **What does a football coach help you get good at?**
- **What does a singing coach help you get good at?**
- **What does a swimming coach help you get good at?**
- **What does a netball coach help you get good at?**

So, what does a kindness coach help you get good at? You've got it. I help Kind Kids like YOU get better at being kind to yourself, others and the world.

Along my journey of kindness, I have worked with thousands of Kind Kids like you, perhaps ten thousand of them, and worked in hundreds of schools throughout the UK. Not bad! Guess what I found along the way? We all share the same goal: to feel happier more of the time, and less sad or worried.

It is important, isn't it, to practise being kind? Good... you and I are on the same page. How do I know that we are on the same page? Because here you are reading my Happy Tank book!

I am glad you agree, because it is my mission to coach YOU by teaching you how to fill your Happy Tank every day. I will take you on a magical journey and coach you on how to make new, daily, *happy habits* and understand how *practice makes progress*. We'll look at the word practice later together.

One of the many things you are really going to like about reading this book is how quickly you can be happier in the day, from practising and making a daily commitment to filling your Happy Tank.

Lots of Kind Kids have told me that my book has changed their lives. How exciting! They also said it is easy to carry out the exercises. I know reading this book will help you and that the sooner you start practising, the sooner you will have more happiness in your life.

You can also visit my YouTube channel, Kindness Matters TV, and find the section entitled *The Happy Tank*, where we can practise the exercises together with lots of other Kind Kids to support our mental health and wellbeing.

UNDERSTANDING YOUR HABITS AND MOOD

OXYGEN MASK

Have you ever been on a plane? Whether you have or not, I want to share what I have noticed on planes – not children picking their noses and eating their bogies, or being naughty, although I have seen that – but the cabin crew doing their announcements. As well as telling people what time food is served (my favourite part), the crew give out safety measures, and describe what you have to do if the cabin loses pressure or the plane falls out of the sky. I do hope you are not reading this book whilst sitting on a plane!

The announcement goes something like this:

'In the unlikely event of a loss of cabin pressure, oxygen masks will drop down from the panels above your head. Pull the mask towards you, place it firmly over your nose and mouth, and breathe normally. Secure your own mask before helping others'.

For the record, I'd definitely need a mask if a plane dropped thousands of feet from the sky. I can guarantee there would be a terrible smell coming from my pants (I think you know why)! What I like about the flight announcement, and not doing a poo in my pants, is that by putting your own mask on first, you take care of yourself and then you are ready to help those around you. In other words, if you take care of your mental health and wellbeing first, you are more capable of bringing happiness to those you love.

Most of my Kind Kids have admitted they rarely stick to doing something every day to be kind to their mental health and wellbeing. That causes lots of unhappiness in their life. Don't get me wrong, I am a kindness coach and love being kind, but you have to do what my Kind Kids and I do. You have to start with yourself by filling your Happy Tank every single morning. Once your Happy Tank is full, you can then share your happiness with everyone throughout the day and when you get home, refill your tank again. Eat, sleep and repeat every day!

However, there is one big problem we have to get out of the way, as it can steal your happiness. That is your UNHELPFUL HABITS!

I wonder what unhelpful habits you have? Which habits are stopping you from filling your Happy Tank each morning? Turn the page and find out!

KNOW YOUR UNHELPFUL HABITS

HABITS ARE A PART OF EVERYDAY LIFE.
SOME ARE HELPFUL AND
KEEP US CHUGGING ALONG,
OTHERS ARE NOT SO HELPFUL!

What are some unhelpful habits?

- Picking your nose. And please don't say you eat it! YUCK!

- Not putting your hand over your mouth when you yawn.

- Leaving your dirty clothes on the bedroom floor.

- Going to bed late.

- Breaking wind.*

*Side note: breaking wind is not an unhelpful habit in itself, it just depends where you do it! For the record, breaking wind in bed is perfectly normal. I remember when I was a Kind Kid, I had extra beans on toast for dinner and as the saying goes... *Beans are good for your heart, the more you eat the more you... get smart!* I woke up the next morning and my duvet was on the other side of the bed. It must have been really windy that night! Okay, less talk about breaking wind – back to the story and how we create happy habits.

GUESS HOW LONG IT TAKES TO START TO CREATE A NEW HABIT? 21 DAYS!

GUESS HOW LONG IT TAKES TO START TO BREAK AN UNHELPFUL HABIT? 21 DAYS!

REALLY, JOHN?

Apparently, it takes around 21 days to create or break a habit, which means that after 22 days of daily *practice*, you will be a proper kindness coach like meeee, John Mageeee!

Snoozy Woozy Sleeping Suzie and Nate, Nate, Going to Bed Late

Now, first off we need to think about some unhelpful habits that might stop us from filling our Happy Tank every morning. Are you sitting comfortably in your chair, you amazing, cool, Kind Kid? Let's start this section with a story.

Once upon a time in a sunny seaside town called Blackpool, where they sell toffee rock, sweets and candy floss, lived a year 5 girl called Snoozy Woozy Sleeping Suzie and a year 5 boy called Nate, Nate, Going To Bed Late. Both children were ecstatic to start *The Happy Tank* with the rest of their Kind Kid friends. But, there was a problem. Their unhelpful habits meant that Snoozy Woozy Sleeping Suzie and Nate, Nate, Going To Bed Late would often forget to wake up 15 minutes before their alarm, unlike the rest of their class, to practise filling their Happy Tank.

Suzie and Nate had very similar habits and told the rest of their class about them. The Kind Kids found that they too wanted to share stories about their unhelpful habits.

Suzie's unhelpful habits

7:00 AM

I woke up late because I kept snoozing my alarm and going back to sleep.

7:15 AM

I rushed to the bathroom but could not shower, because my sister was already in there.

7:30 AM

There was no time left for breakfast, so I grabbed a piece of toast and ran to the car. My mum was upset and gave me that look (you know the one). She was worried I was going to make her late for work.

7:45 AM

I was so busy rushing around that I forgot my pencil case, homework and lunch box. I think I might have forgotten my head if it were not on top of my shoulders.

8:00 AM

Mum revved up the car, and I reached school smelling like a pig, feeling hungry and very sulky!

Nate's unhelpful habits

7:00 AM

I woke up late because I had stayed up playing Fortnite on my Xbox®. When I did go to bed I couldn't sleep because my brain was rushing with ideas about the game.

7:15 AM

I only had time for a quick face wash. I looked like I had been dragged through a garden bush backwards.

7:30 AM

There was no time left for breakfast which made me grumpy. We all know breakfast is the most important meal of the day and my stomach was rumbling all the way to school, where luckily I got fruit and toast from the breakfast club. Thank goodness for the breakfast club!

7:45 AM

I was really upset, as I had forgotten my swimming trunks, so I was unable to enjoy a swimming lesson with my friends that afternoon.

8:00 AM

**I forgot my spelling book and reading glasses and felt like
I had let myself and my teacher down, who was helping me
to get really good at my spellings.**

Becoming aware of your own unhelpful habits

What are your unhelpful habits? In the box below, write down a few things that could prevent you from getting up 15 minutes before your normal alarm to fill up your Happy Tank. Some of your answers may be similar to Snoozy Woozy Sleeping Suzie and Nate, Nate, Going To Bed Late. Remember it is perfectly normal to have unhelpful habits, we all have them!

*I might not have time to fill
my Happy Tank in the morning
because...*

....
....
....
....
....
....
....

CREATING HAPPY HABITS

HAS IT EVER OCCURRED TO YOU THAT BY MAKING A FEW SMALL CHANGES TO YOUR DAILY HABITS, YOUR LIFE COULD CHANGE FOR THE BETTER FOREVER? HOW COOL!

What are some helpful habits?

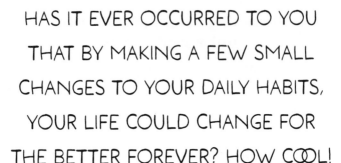

- Going to bed on time.
- Being kind to others.
- Practising your spellings.
- Putting your dirty clothes in the washing basket.
- Brushing your teeth before bedtime.

Now let's look at some fantastic examples of new happy habits that help us fill our Happy Tank each morning.

Here is Brilliant Billie's amazing example of how she fills her Happy Tank every day:

THE NIGHT BEFORE:

• I take a shower.

• I prepare my school bag and place it neatly by the front door.

• I read a book until I'm ready to fall asleep.

• I set my alarm 15 minutes earlier than normal or I ask my parents/carers to wake me up 15 minutes earlier than normal.

IN THE MORNING:

6:45 AM
When told it is time for school I bounce out of bed, use the bathroom and wash my face with cold water.

7:00 AM
I sit on my bed, on the floor or in a chair in my bedroom and begin to fill my Happy Tank.

7:15 AM

I skip down the stairs with a big smile on my face to have some breakfast.

7:30 AM

I double-check I have everything that I packed the night before.

7:45 AM

I get in the car with my mum and I have a large smile on my face. I get to school early and tell my teacher I have filled my Happy Tank. I practise filling my Happy Tank again with my class.

In the box below, write down a few things that you could do to help with your morning routine.

> ## *What positive changes could I make to my morning routine?....*
>
> ....
> ....
> ....
> ....
> ....
> ....
> ....
> ....
> ....
> ....
> ....

Keeping happy habits

Think about these daily habits:

- Brushing your hair.

- Brushing your teeth.

- Washing your hands.

- Getting dressed.

- Eating your food.

All of the previous activities you do without thinking, because you have made them into a daily habit. So, if you can master daily habits like these, it will be easy peasy lemon squeezy to learn new ones to fill your Happy Tank, won't it?

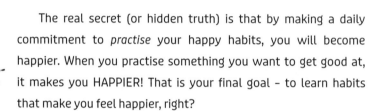

The real secret (or hidden truth) is that by making a daily commitment to *practise* your happy habits, you will become happier. When you practise something you want to get good at, it makes you HAPPIER! That is your final goal – to learn habits that make you feel happier, right?

When amazing Kind Kids like you want to get better at something, they practise every day, don't they? The key to overcoming your unhelpful habits is *PRACTISE, PRACTISE, PRACTISE = PROGRESS!* Go gentle with yourself and keep practising daily. Before you know it, you will have created happy habits.

THE MOOD METER!

I love teaching the Mood Meter to Kind Kids just like you because, I kid you not, the Mood Meter is a great way to learn how to be aware of your feelings, how to love and accept them and how to change them.

Take a look at the Mood Meter. If I am ever feeling like a number 2 – and I'm not talking here about the loo – I can do something about it. The first thing is to accept how you are

— 10 AWESOME
— 9 ECSTATIC
— 8 GREAT
— 7 HAPPY
— 6 CONTENT
— 5 OK
— 4 WORRIED
— 3 ANXIOUS
— 2 SAD
— 1 ANGRY

feeling and understand what type of feeling it is, then look for an opportunity to do an act of kindness for someone else. It could mean giving a compliment, helping the teacher tidy the classroom, helping someone who is upset, making someone feel included, or asking them if they want to play.

You will notice that your feelings change from bad to good by helping someone else feel happy with your kindness. What you do comes back to you. Kindness is like a boomerang: when you are kind to others and make them happy, it comes back to you just like a boomerang. This is a great way to manage your feelings and emotions.

KINDNESS IS LIKE A BOOMERANG

I wonder what acts of kindness you could do when feeling upset, worried, angry or any other unhelpful feeling, to change your Mood Meter?

Write down three acts of kindness you could do that would make you feel better if you were ever upset:

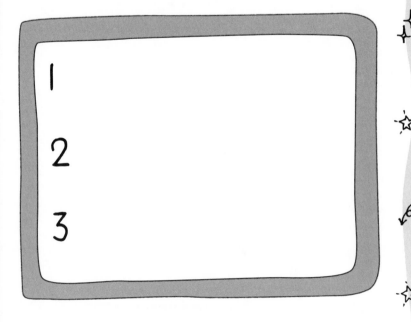

1

2

3

I can't wait to share with you what you can do to take your Mood Meter to a 10 every day.

I hope you are ready to start the magical journey of a lifetime and learn how to fill your Happy Tank daily. As I said, I swear on my cat's life, as long as you *practise, practise, practise* daily, your life is going to be filled with so much happiness. I imagine that if you are still reading my book then you also like to practise, don't you?

SIX WAYS TO FILL YOUR HAPPY TANK

BREATHING

JUST KEEP BREATHING.
ONE BREATH IN,
ONE BREATH OUT.

As I write this section, I want to remind you that practising your breathing can help you feel calm, relaxed and happy.

Whether you are filling your Happy Tank at home, in your class or during a school assembly, one of the many things you're really going to like about these six exercises is that you are giving kindness to yourself.

Remember, you are going to learn six new ways to fill your Happy Tank, that will make you feel more calm and relaxed. Here is the first way and I will move onto the next five in the next chapters of the book. I am going to break down each activity for you. Do you know why? Because it is the kind thing to do, and kindness matters!

Let's make sure you are on the ball. Remember the story I shared about knowing your unhelpful habits? (Revisit page 30 if you need to.) This time we are going to write a list of anything that could distract us before we go on to complete our breathing exercise. Afterwards, look at the to-do list for the exercise.

Know your unhelpful habits: Distractions

List out anything around you that could distract you from filling your Happy Tank and then make sure you do not let those things prevent you from completing your breathing exercise. You've got this!

....
....
....
....
....
....
....
....
....
....

My Happy Tank to-do list:

- Sit on your bed, chair or the floor.

- Set a timer for two minutes.

- Close your eyes and begin your breathing time.

Let's do this!

Before starting the exercise, take some regular, deep breaths to prepare yourself and get relaxed. I like to do three of these deep breaths. Close your eyes, take a deep breath in and let it out. Again, take a deep breath in and let it out. One more time take a deep breath in, and then let it out.

Now, we are going to breathe in and out while counting to ten. If your mind begins to wander, and that would be perfectly normal, go back to number one and start counting again. It's surprising how many ideas can pop into your head – sometimes I catch myself thinking of fish fingers, chips and beans, eating sweets, watching YouTube, but I never give up. Instead, I patiently go back to my first breath.

Don't give yourself a hard time if you think of different things and forget what number you are on. Remember, it is the

1... 2...
3... 4... 5...
6... 7... 8...
9... 10...

nature of your mind to think. Think of your thoughts as fluffy clouds passing by; let them come and go because behind those clouds is the sunshine and that sunshine is you.

Close your eyes and begin:

> **Breathe in and silently say to yourself, 'One'**
>
> **Breathe out and silently say to yourself, 'Two'**
>
> **Breathe in and silently say to yourself, 'Three'**
>
> **Breathe out and silently say to yourself, 'Four'**
>
> **Breathe in and silently say to yourself, 'Five'**
>
> **Breathe out and silently say to yourself, 'Six'**
>
> **Breathe in and silently say to yourself, 'Seven'**
>
> **Breathe out and silently say to yourself, 'Eight'**
>
> **Breathe in and silently say to yourself, 'Nine'**
>
> **Breathe out and silently say to yourself, 'Ten'**

Keep repeating this until you have completed two minutes of the breathing exercise.

Now flip the page and you can learn about the next level of filling your Happy Tank, 'Reflection'. Let's get into some reflection time.

Wim Hof

Have you ever heard the name Wim Hof before? Better known as The Iceman, he is a famous Dutch athlete and speaker who has set records for swimming under ice, withstanding extreme freezing temperatures and running a half-marathon on the snow barefoot. Every day, he practises cold exposure, breathing techniques, yoga and meditation. His famous breathing techniques allow him to stay calm and more relaxed under extreme temperatures.

Research the Wim Hof Method online. Find out three more interesting facts about this incredible athlete and write them below:

1

2

3

REFLECTION

ITS A BEAUTIFUL THING FOR YOUR MIND
TO TAKE SOME TIME TO REFLECT
EVERY DAY.

Have you ever looked at yourself in the mirror and noticed your beautiful face gazing back at you? Well, that's your beautiful reflection! But reflection has another meaning too. For example, when was the last time you *reflected* on your choices? Or last time you reflected full stop? It may have been at school or at home.

Generally speaking, making time to reflect can help you to consider your choices and experiences. You may be used to reflecting on choices you regret or choices that made you happy. You may focus on the present, or the near or distant past. Whatever you choose to do with your reflection time is yours alone to decide, and no matter what comes up, it is an opportunity to think about what you may or may not want to do differently or what you may feel grateful for.

Let me share a trick I do: I close my eyes and feel calm and relaxed. I focus on breathing, following my breath, and when a thought comes to mind I silently say to myself, "What could I do differently?". I then wait and see what jumps into my head.

Sometimes a thought comes up, and at other times it doesn't. Both are okay. What's important is that you keep your eyes closed, relax and let your mind wander and let your amazing creative imagination do its thing.

Here's how you can practise your reflection time:

What could I have done differently?

Slowly breathe in and out, and allow your mind to wander. When a thought pops into your head write it down and then have a good think about how/if you would change this thought. I've left some examples to show you how it's done.

A thought that came in to my mind was...
e.g. I am doing very well practising filling my Happy Tank daily.
e.g. Why did I snap at my friend earlier?

....
....
....
....
....

Now think, what could I have done differently? Write some ideas in the space below.
e.g. I could possibly watch less YouTube and practise filling my Happy Tank more.
e.g. I could have apologised to my friend after I snapped at them, so I will say sorry when I next see them.

....
....
....
....
....

DID YOU KNOW?

Beyoncé Knowles

Whether you love her music or aren't a fan, Beyoncé Knowles has become famous all over the world for her chart-topping albums, fashion brands, perfumes, charity work and public appearances. As well as being a multi-millionaire pop star and fashion icon, Beyoncé has learned to recognise the need to take care of herself, take time off and meditate between touring and recording. She wakes up every morning at six to start her day off with mindfulness and self-reflection. This helps her to perform to the standard she does, and push herself more every day. Find out three interesting facts about this incredible singer and write them in the list below:

1

2

3

KINDNESS

IF YOUR KINDNESS DOES NOT INCLUDE YOURSELF, IT IS INCOMPLETE

I would like you to reflect (see what I did there) on the last act of kindness you carried out. I imagine you can probably recall a generous act you carried out for someone else. That is great – thank you for your kindness. However, when was the last time you did something kind to or for yourself? If you are like me and lots of others, you probably forget to be kind towards yourself. Remember the story I shared about the oxygen mask on page 26-27? I am not saying for one minute that it is not important to be kind to others, because it is, but it is vitally important to be kind to ourselves *first*! In this section of *The Happy Tank*, that's exactly what we are going to learn. You are going to *start with yourself*. There are five stages in this section:

1. **Kindness towards yourself.**
2. **Kindness towards friends, family or pets (things we love and respect).**
3. **Kindness towards others (a member of the community or someone you only know by face).**
4. **Kindness towards someone who has been unkind to you (forgiveness).**
5. **Kindness towards all living things.**

Work through the stages, and try out the exercise for each one:

<u>STAGE ONE</u>

Kindness towards yourself.

With your eyes closed and focusing on your breath, silently say to yourself, ***"May I be well. May I be happy. May I be OK."*** Love and accept these words of kindness to yourself. Now, move on to stage two.

MAY I BE WELL.
MAY I BE HAPPY.
MAY I BE OK.

STAGE TWO

Kindness towards friends, family or pets.

Once you have given kindness to yourself, with your eyes still closed, extend your kindness to others. Think of a family member, a friend or a pet. Think of their names. Say silently in your mind who you want to give your kindness to. Repeat the words in your head, *"May you be well. May you be happy. May you be OK."*

STAGE THREE

Kindness to others.

Show kindness towards a person you know by face. This could be a neighbour, a member of the community, a teacher at school that you don't know that well or a familiar face you see where you do your hobbies.

Think of that person and say silently in your mind, *"May you be well. May you be happy. May you be OK."*

STAGE FOUR

Kindness towards someone who has been unkind to you (forgiveness).

This can sometimes be challenging but thanks to the amazing gift of your imagination, you can practise, practise, practise and make progress forgiving the person who has been unkind. Think of someone who has been unkind to you. Say silently in your mind, ***"May you be well. May you be happy. May you be OK."*** If it gets uncomfortable then go back and repeat stage one first.

STAGE FIVE

Kindness towards all living things.

I love stage five as I get to let my imagination run wilder than a wildebeest. Say silently in your mind, ***"May all living things be well. May all living things be happy. May all living things be OK."***

MAY YOU BE WELL.

MAY YOU BE HAPPY.

MAY YOU BE OK.

Activity time! ♡

Think of three acts of kindness you could do this week and write them below. They could be acts of kindness towards yourself, a friend, a family member, a pet or someone in your school or community.

....

....

....

....

....

....

....

....

....

....

....

....

WOW!

You are an amazing Kind Kid and you are definitely becoming a kindness coach in the making!

WELL DONE.

Greta Thunberg and His Holiness the 14th Dalai Lama

You will probably have heard of Greta Thunberg, the Swedish activist who was just eight years old when she learned about the science of climate change. This made her worried and compelled her to action. Now, she visits leaders from around the globe to make a change to the world we live in. Greta Thunberg met the 14th Dalai Lama in January 2021 via a live stream. They spoke about how to be kinder to the planet and the importance of respect and compassion in everyday life. The Dalai Lama is the spiritual leader of the Tibetan people known to promote non-violence and kindness in Buddhism and beyond. Go online to watch their meeting and see how their habits of sharing kindness have impacted the world we live in. Find out three interesting facts about these important figures and write them in the list below:

1

2

3

WOW!

You are halfway through filling your Happy Tank to the top and you will soon be ready to share your happiness with others, both at school and out in the world. How cool is that?

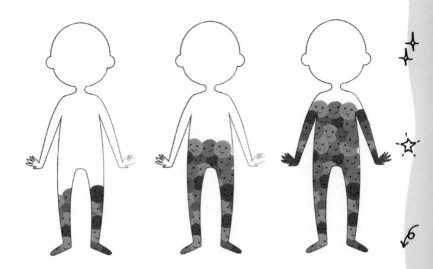

I RECKON YOU'RE ENJOYING FEELING HAPPIER FROM FILLING YOUR HAPPY TANK, AREN'T YOU?

AFFIRMATIONS

FILLING MY HAPPY TANK IS A HAPPY HABIT, AND HAPPY HABITS MAKE ME HAPPY.

Affirmations are sentences that we say and repeat to ourselves to help us feel better. Repeat and practise the affirmation below to feel better...remember practice makes progress.

Sometimes affirmations can help us deal with negative thoughts or experiences, like criticism.

CRITICISM

Noun

The expression of disapproval of someone or something on the basis of perceived faults or mistakes.

A lot of pupils criticise themselves and others. For the record, I beg you to STOP criticising yourself and others. If you make a mistake, then practise the affirmation below and remember you learn more from your mistakes than any results you get in life. The trick is to not repeat the same mistake.

Learn to memorise the affirmation below and with your eyes closed keep repeating it silently to yourself for two minutes. You have got this!

Affirmation:

> "I AM ALWAYS DOING MY BEST
> UNTIL I FIND A BETTER WAY
> OF DOING THINGS."

You are always doing your best. Yes, you will make mistakes – we all do, even I do – but please DO NOT criticise yourself and give yourself a hard time.

Another negative thought that is common with pupils is comparison.

COMPARISON

Noun

A consideration or estimate of the similarities or dissimilarities between two things or people.

To do your best, you should not *compare* yourself to others. You are perfect just the way you are. You do not need to look like or be like anyone else or have things other people have. You would be surprised to know how many people would love to have what you have got and they will even compare themselves to you. We will talk about that in the next section, which is about gratitude. For now, if you notice you are comparing yourself to others or any material objects others have, then affirm to yourself...

Affirmation:

> "COMPARISON IS THE THIEF OF JOY.
> I DO NOT NEED TO COMPARE MYSELF
> TO ANYTHING OR ANYONE."

With your eyes closed, keep repeating the affirmation silently to yourself for two minutes.

If you have privacy, it is okay to say the affirmation out loud if you are comfortable with that. Remember...

PRACTISE, PRACTISE, PRACTISE MAKES PROGRESS.

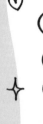

I AM NOT LOOKING FOR PERFECTION, I AM LOOKING FOR PROGRESS

Here are my top ten favourite affirmations that can help with all kinds of thoughts and feelings. Practise, practise, practise = progress. Memorise them and say them to yourself silently throughout the day or out loud when you are in privacy. This will be just like practising your times tables until you become really good at them. You will be amazed how good affirmations can make you feel.

Even better, they are easy peasy lemon squeezy to learn.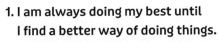

1. I am always doing my best until
   I find a better way of doing things.

2. Comparison is the thief of joy. I do not need to compare myself to anything or anyone.

3. I deeply and completely love and accept myself.

4. I love my friends and family members just as they are.
   I do not try to change anyone.

5. I am no longer curious about things that upset me.

6. I am proud of everything I have already achieved.

7. Today, I look at all the positive things in my life, and
   I am grateful for them all.

8. Today is going to be a really, really good day.

9. I close my eyes, think positive thoughts and breathe goodness in and out.

10. I am looking forward to what is ahead.

Try these affirmations out during your two minutes of practice for this exercise, or you can come up with your own positive affirmations!

Louise Hay

You may not have heard of Louise Hay. She is famous for having written books in the United States of America about the power of changing negative thoughts into positive affirmations. I was an adult when I first came across her work in 2010 and bought her book *You Can Heal Your Life* for one of my children, Millie. Together, we read the book and it taught us about the extraordinary importance of practising affirmations to heal and transform lives for the better. Go online and find your three favourite affirmations that you can start using, and write them in the list below:

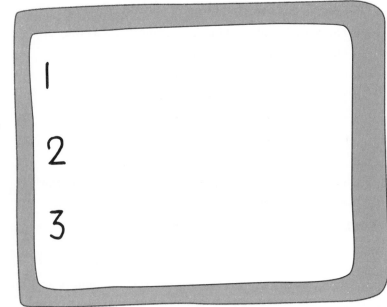

1

2

3

GRATITUDE

THE BEST WAY TO START
AND END A DAY
IS WITH A GRATEFUL HEART.

D id you know that you can't be unhappy and grateful at the time? "Say what, John?" It's true, you can't. Go back to the Mood Meter on page 39 and if you ever find yourself on a number 3 or lower, then the question I want you to ask yourself is...

WHAT AM I GRATEFUL FOR RIGHT NOW?

There are so many things that you could be grateful for in your life. You could be grateful for the people around you who make you feel happy, so the answer to the question above could be, *"I am grateful for **my friends**"*. Or it could be for something really exciting that you own that brings you lots of joy, *"I am grateful for **my Xbox®**"*. You could be grateful for amazing skills you have, *"I am grateful that **I have a beautiful singing voice**"*. The list could go on and on, if you really think hard about it.

I AM GRATEFUL FOR
MY FRIENDS

Now you can have a go at finishing the sentences below with what YOU are grateful for.

I AM GRATEFUL FOR..............

....

....

....

I AM GRATEFUL FOR..............

....

....

....

I AM GRATEFUL FOR..............

....

....

....

I AM GRATEFUL FOR..............

....

....

....

I AM GRATEFUL FOR..............

....

....

....

....

I AM GRATEFUL FOR..............

....
....
....

I AM GRATEFUL FOR..............

....
....
....

I AM GRATEFUL FOR..............

....
....
....

I AM GRATEFUL FOR..............

....
....
....

I AM GRATEFUL FOR..............

....
....
....

With your eyes closed for two minutes, keep saying to yourself as many things as you can that you are grateful for.

2:00

When you say what you are grateful for, really begin to feel the emotion and think about how having all the things you are grateful for makes you feel. There are so many things to be grateful for and gratitude helps us focus on the positive rather than the negative.

If you ever feel upset at any time of the day, notice and reflect on how you feel in that moment and then stop yourself and ask,

WHAT AM I GRATEFUL FOR RIGHT NOW?"

I swear on my cat's life you will start to feel better in no time. (I loved that cat. It was a good cat, I knew I should've never named it Lucky, lol 🙂 .)

Activity time!

Think of a person who you would love to say a big 'thank you' to. It could be a friend, a family member, a teacher... anyone in your life! Maybe they taught you something new recently, they helped you with homework, or they really made you laugh when you needed it. Imagine you are writing them a thank you note, what would you say? Write it down in the space below.

....

....

....

....

....

....

....

....

....

....

....

....

....

....

....

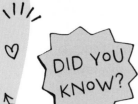
DID YOU KNOW?

Kid President

Robby Novak is known to millions as Kid President, the YouTube sensation. He was 11 when he first shared his videos online. His Kid President character loves corn dogs and basketball, and he has even given Beyoncé Knowles a kiss on the cheek! Together, he and his brother-in-law have been on a mission to inspire kids and grown-ups to make the world a better place. He rose to fame in his black suit and red tie, spreading messages of gratitude, happiness and love. Watch the following Kid President videos on YouTube and think about the advice that is given.

- Kid President's 20 Things We Should Say More Often
- Kid President's 25 Reasons To Be Thankful!
- A Pep Talk from Kid President to You

Write down your three favourite pieces of advice in the list below:

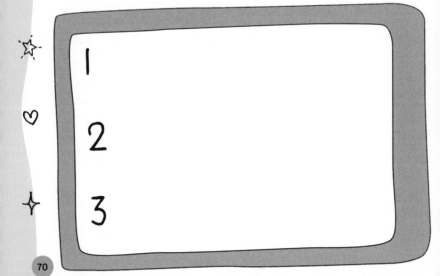

1

2

3

HAPPY TAPPING
– (EFT – EMOTIONALLY FOCUSED THERAPY)

HAPPINESS IS WHEN
WHAT YOU THINK,
WHAT YOU SAY, AND WHAT YOU DO
ARE IN HARMONY.
Mahatma Gandhi

OMGGG, oh my good, golly, gosh! You are on the final stage of filling your Happy Tank. I am super proud of you and I hope you are proud of all your practice.

I have to confess that lots of pupils find Happy Tapping good fun. Sometimes it can take a while to get good at it, but remember it's all about practice, practice, practice, so after 21 days you will be amazing. You could also visit my YouTube channel, Kindness Matters TV and look for Happy Tapping, and you will find me along with lots of Kind Kids like you practising their Happy Tapping.

So, come on John, what is this Happy Tapping and how do we get good at it? I am glad you want to know, so here we go!

There are nine tapping points on your body. They are:

1. Left hand (karate chop hand)

2. Above your eyebrows

3. Side of your eyes

4. Under your eyes

5. Under your nose

6. Chin

7. Collarbone – the bone between the top of your chest and shoulder

8. Under your arm (rib cage)

9. Top of your head

Now follow the steps below, tapping as you repeat the sentences.

STEP 1

Look at the Mood Meter on page 39. How do you feel?

10 = Awesome   **1= Angry**

Let's use 'worried' as our example. Ready? Let's go!

STEP 2

Tap on the karate chop point (side of your left hand), start tapping and say two times:

"EVEN THOUGH I FEEL WORRIED, I DEEPLY
AND COMPLETELY LOVE AND ACCEPT MYSELF"

STEP 3

Say each sentence in the right-hand column below twice, while tapping on the point shown in the left-hand column. Then move onto the next sentence.

Tap on this point	Say out loud
Above your eyebrows	I feel worried.
Side of your eyes	I am overthinking.
Under your eyes	I want to stop overthinking.
Under your nose	Why do I worry?
Chin	I don't like worrying.
Collarbone	I feel unsettled and worried.
Under your arm	I am so tired of feeling this way.
Top of your head	Worrying does not help me.

STEP 4

Time for round two! Again, say each sentence in the right-hand column twice, while tapping on the point shown in the left-hand column. Then move onto the next sentence.

Tap on this point	Say out loud
Above your eyebrows	It's normal to worry.
Side of your eyes	Everybody worries.
Under your eyes	I can choose to think happy thoughts.
Under your nose	Happy thoughts make me happy.
Chin	I am feeling happier.
Collarbone	Happy Tapping makes me happy.
Under your arm	Now I feel good.
Top of your head	Now I feel calm and happy.

STEP 5

Close your eyes for a moment or two and focus on your breathing.

STEP 6

Open your eyes and take a deep breath in and breathe out and say

"I AM SAFE. ALL IS WELL."

Then open your Happy Tapping hands and release all your happiness.

STEP 7

Go to page 39 to look again at the Mood Meter. On a scale of 1-10, how do you feel now?

YOU DID AMAZINGLY WELL.
I AM PROUD OF YOU!

DID YOU KNOW?

Whoopi Goldberg

You may have seen the film *Sister Act* and the incredible Whoopi Goldberg in action. She is an actor and producer, who started to act when she was only eight in a children's theatre company. She spent her early years in a Manhattan housing project and turned her life around by facing her fears and practising the Happy Tapping technique (or EFT, Emotionally Focused Therapy). Whoopi uses this technique most when needing to fly to stage productions and film sets. She recently opened up about her previous fear of flying and how EFT helped her to overcome that fear and allowed her to make her way to London 12 years ago when she first worked on *Sister Act*. If you have not seen the film, why not ask your parent or carer if you can check it out online? It spreads a message of inclusion, kindness and joy to those who watch it. You can also learn more about how Happy Tapping (EFT) has helped Whoopi and so many others to overcome their fears. Write three things below that you enjoyed about your Happy Tapping exercise.

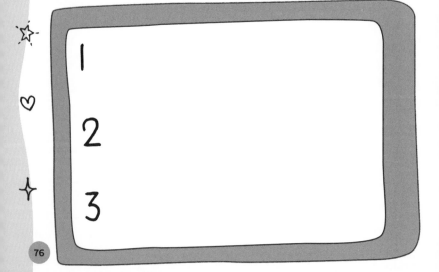

1

2

3

THE
CHALLENGE

THE
HAPPY TANK
CHALLENGE

I AM FILLING MY LIFE
WITH HAPPY HABITS
BECAUSE HAPPY HABITS
MAKE ME HAPPY!

Seeing as you have made it this far, I thought you would be up for a challenge. Are you up for it? What's that, I hear you say? A big yes? Cool, let's do this!

To form new happy habits, you must practise, practise, practise because, as you now know...

PRACTICE = PROGRESS

Remember, we are learning how to create daily happy habits. Once you have completed your Happy Tank Challenge, here is what you will receive: a fantastic Happy Tank certificate! Ask an adult to visit www.kindnessmatters.co.uk/thehappytank to get your certificate. They're really cool!

On the next page is your Challenge Tracker to track your daily/ weekly progress.

This is a great way to make you feel good about yourself and reflect and see all your progress. If you miss a day by any chance, go easy on yourself and chill your beans. Life can be unpredictable! Just get back on the horse the next day (and when I say get back on the horse, that is just a figure of speech).

Just try your hardest to practise every day by yourself, with a friend or an adult, or practise along with me on my YouTube channel. Remember to tick your tracker every day that you practise.

Here we go; hold on tight.

The Challenge Tracker

We are going to focus on one exercise each week, and you need to practise the exercise every day if you can – go on, you can do it!

WEEK ONE

This week we are going to focus on:

Breathing

Each day, before you begin, repeat this sentence to yourself:

> "TODAY, I AM 100% COMMITTED
> TO FILLING MY HAPPY TANK."

Go back to page 44 if you need a reminder about how to do your breathing exercise.

Tick the box next to each day that you practise your breathing.

- 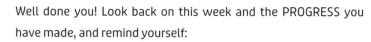 **Monday**
- **Tuesday**
- **Wednesday**
- **Thursday**
- **Friday**
- **Saturday**
- **Sunday**

Well done you! Look back on this week and the PROGRESS you have made, and remind yourself:

> "WE ARE NOT LOOKING FOR PERFECTION;
> WE ARE LOOKING FOR PROGRESS".

WEEK TWO

This week we are going to focus on:

Reflection

Each day, before you begin, repeat this sentence to yourself:

> "TODAY, I AM 100% COMMITTED
> TO FILLING MY HAPPY TANK."

Go back to page 49 if you need a reminder about how to do your reflection exercise.

Tick the box next to each day that you practise reflection.

- **Monday**
- **Tuesday**
- **Wednesday**
- **Thursday**
- **Friday**
- **Saturday**
- **Sunday**

Well done you! Look back on this week and the PROGRESS you have made, and remind yourself:

> "WE ARE NOT LOOKING FOR PERFECTION;
> WE ARE LOOKING FOR PROGRESS".

WEEK THREE

This week we are going to focus on:

Kindness

Each day, before you begin, repeat this sentence to yourself:

> "TODAY, I AM 100% COMMITTED
> TO FILLING MY HAPPY TANK."

Go back to page 53 if you need a reminder about how to do your kindness exercise.

Tick the box next to each day that you practise kindness.

- ☀ **Monday**
- ☀ **Tuesday**
- ☀ **Wednesday**
- ☀ **Thursday**
- ☀ **Friday**
- ☀ **Saturday**
- ☀ **Sunday**

Well done you, you've now completed 21 days of the challenge! This means you are well on your way to forming those daily happy habits.

Look back on this week and the PROGRESS you have made, and remind yourself:

> "WE ARE NOT LOOKING FOR PERFECTION;
> WE ARE LOOKING FOR PROGRESS".

WEEK FOUR

This week we are going to focus on:

Affirmations

Each day, before you begin, repeat this sentence to yourself:

> "TODAY, I AM 100% COMMITTED
> TO FILLING MY HAPPY TANK."

Go back to page 60 if you need a reminder about how to do your affirmation exercise.

Tick the box next to each day that you practise your affirmations.

- ☼ **Monday**
- ☼ **Tuesday**
- ☼ **Wednesday**
- ☼ **Thursday**
- ☼ **Friday**
- ☼ **Saturday**
- ☼ **Sunday**

Well done you! Look back on this week and the PROGRESS you have made, and remind yourself:

> "WE ARE NOT LOOKING FOR PERFECTION;
> WE ARE LOOKING FOR PROGRESS".

WEEK FIVE

This week we are going to focus on:

Gratitude

Each day, before you begin, repeat this sentence to yourself:

> "TODAY, I AM 100% COMMITTED
> TO FILLING MY HAPPY TANK."

Go back to page 65 if you need a reminder about how to do your gratitude exercise.

Tick the box next to each day that you practise gratitude.

- ☀ **Monday**
- ☀ **Tuesday**
- ☀ **Wednesday**
- ☀ **Thursday**
- ☀ **Friday**
- ☀ **Saturday**
- ☀ **Sunday**

Well done you! Look back on this week and the PROGRESS you have made, and remind yourself:

> "WE ARE NOT LOOKING FOR PERFECTION;
> WE ARE LOOKING FOR PROGRESS".

WEEK SIX

This week we are going to focus on:

Happy Tapping

Each day, before you begin, repeat this sentence to yourself:

"TODAY, I AM 100% COMMITTED
TO FILLING MY HAPPY TANK."

Go back to page 71 if you need a reminder about how to do your Happy Tapping exercise.

Tick the box next to each day that you practise your Happy Tapping.

- **Monday**
- **Tuesday**
- **Wednesday**
- **Thursday**
- **Friday**
- **Saturday**
- **Sunday**

Well done you! Look back on this week and the PROGRESS you have made, and remind yourself:

"WE ARE NOT LOOKING FOR PERFECTION;
WE ARE LOOKING FOR PROGRESS".

CONGRATULATIONS!

WELL DONE, YOU HAVE MADE IT!
I AM SO PROUD OF YOU,
AND I HAVE THE BIGGEST SMILE
ON MY FACE.

Now you can practise filling your Happy Tank every day and being kind to yourself, walking around with a big grin. I wonder, who could you teach the Happy Tank to? Imagine how good you would feel if you were to teach a friend what you have learnt, or you could even set up a Happy Tank room at school. How cool would that be? You could ask a teacher at school if you could use a section of the library or a quiet room where you could help other children who may feel upset.

You could all practise filling your Happy Tanks together or set up an after-school Happy Tank Club! This could be a great way to teach others everything that you have learnt. There is no right or wrong way to do this; you can create a space that works best for you and other pupils to fill your Happy Tanks in.

To get your Happy Tank certificates, ask an adult to visit my website www.kindnessmatters.co.uk/thehappytank

I look forward to you and all the other Kind Kids in my Kindness Crew joining me on my YouTube channel: Kindness Matters TV. Feel free to comment and let me know how you are doing each day with your Happy Tank.

Thank you for your kindness and for taking the time to read and apply *The Happy Tank*; although I have never met you in person, I hope the book will help to support your mental health and wellbeing, whether you are a child, teacher or adult.

Thank you for your kindness,

JOHN MAGEE

The Kindness Coach

PEOPLE TO FOLLOW

Headteachers, members of SLT, and teaching staff, I highly recommend you explore the works of the following exceptional educators and consider booking them to support your pupils and staff with regard to their mental health and wellbeing. I have included their Twitter handles and websites below:

Tom Percival
http://tom-percival.com
Twitter @TomPercivalsays

FlyHighBillie
www.flyhighbillie.org
Twitter @flyhighbillie_

Ben Brown
www.educationroundtables.co.uk
Twitter @EdRoundtables

Gaurav and Divya Garg
www.letslocalise.co.uk
Twitter @LetsLocalise

Andrew Cowley
Twitter @andrew_cowley23

Adrian Bethune
www.teachappy.co.uk
Twitter @AdrianBethune

Toria Bono
www.tinyvoicetalks.com
Twitter @TinyVoiceTalks

Rock Kids
www.rockkidzonline.com
Twitter @RockKidzUK

Action Jackson
www.fixupseminars.co.uk
Twitter @Actionjackson

Nicola Owen
www.zennicwellbeing.co.uk
Twitter @sphoenix78

Paul McGee
www.thesumoguy.com
Twitter @TheSumoGuy @SUMO4Schools

Tom Palmer
www.tompalmer.co.uk
Twitter @tompalmerauthor

Matt Dechaine
www.mattdechaine.com
Twitter @mattdechaine

Drew Povey
www.drewpovey.co.uk
Twitter @drewpovey

Chris Dyson
Twitter @chrisdysonHT

Paul Garvey
www.quality-schools.com
Twitter @PaulGarvey4

ACKNoWLEDGEMENTS

Arthur Luke, for his friendship and for inspiring me to create content to resonate with the pupils I teach.

Esther Smith, for being the best English teacher I know and consistently pushing me to grow.

Mike Kawula, my American accountability partner, for his closeness and for always helping me discern my blind spots.

Chris and Glenda Grimsley, inspiring NLP teachers, for their humility, coaching and friendship.

Neil Bramwell from sunny Melbourne, Australia, for never failing to believe in me and giving up valuable time to share ideas on Zoom.

Tom Percival for his friendship, time and help and solid advice to support my dream of being a children's author.

Aaron Dunleavey for bringing *The Happy Tank* to life with his amazing creative ideas.

Twitter Tribe

Headteacher Claire Jones, for setting up the Twitter Tribe – a safe space to discover how to best shape the next generation of pupils in schools.

Ben Brown from Education Roundtables, a gentleman, for his accountability and support to countless headteachers, which in turn helps them create amazing schools with happy staff and pupils.

Kind Kate Sturdy, for her friendship and for suggesting ways to improve my narrative to better inspire children. Thank you for your kindness.

My Twitter friends, for your support, loyalty and courage, and for making me wake up each day feeling blessed.

Veronica Simster, for providing excellent EFT scripts that transform thousands of pupils' lives throughout the UK with the Happy Tapping.

Adriane Bethune, Andrew Cowley, Action Jackson, Professor Paul McGee, Drew Povey, Tom Palmer, Kyrstie Stubbs, Laura Robson and Nicola Owen, for carving time out of their busy schedules to support me and this book. The difference you make is phenomenal and a privilege to witness and share in.

Westminster Primary Academy

Executive Headteacher Roger Farley, members of SLT, TAs and year 6 cohort of 2021 – to Briony, Johnny, Zara, Scott, Mackenzie, and Sophie, in particular, for their commitment to my book and transforming pupils' mental health and wellbeing in the process. Who would have thought their own stories and experience in lockdown would have helped shape such life-transforming work? I am eternally grateful for their trust.

Unity Academy Blackpool

Headteacher Stephen Cooke, legend Karen Linney, Mandy Hammond and the whole staff (first Kindness Academy in the Galaxy), for friendship, efforts to support external education providers, and allowing pupils to get the support they need to flourish and enjoy their future.

FCAT NLE Executive Headteacher Chris Lickiss, a great man, for forming our working partnership in 2012, which helped me and the Kindness Matters team to transform thousands of pupils' lives in Unity Academy and across Blackpool.

Roy Blake, a friend and mentor, for helping me transform the lives of thousands of children in Blackpool, is a true Kindness Matters ambassador.

Armfield Academy

Headteacher Mark Kilmurray and Deputy Headteacher Janette Webster, Sandra, and Chris for three incredible years of collaboration and especially the stars of *The Happy Tank* – Abbie and Amy.

Blackpool Gateway Academy

Headteacher Alicia Gibbons and the incredible teacher Yasmin Hinds, for helping me develop the Happy Tapping for all year 5 pupils and experiencing the impact it had on their mental health and wellbeing.

Blackpool FC Community Trust

CEO Ashley Hackett, Simon Smith, MJ, Jen and their fantastic staff, for making a big difference in the lives of every child in Blackpool and enabling them to access a copy of *The Happy Tank*.

Blackpool Council

Assistant Director at Blackpool Borough Council, Paul Turner, and Chloe Pieri, for their working partnership and proactive approach to getting all of our Kindness Matters resources into schools to support children's development.

Saint Antony's RC Primary

Headteacher Heather McGowan and all her magnificent staff, for supporting the work I do and implementing the book into the heart of the curriculum.

Blackburn with Darwen Borough Council SIG 5

Blackburn with Darwen SIG 5 School Improvement Group, for their kindness and proactive approach to sharing our educational resources with all the children in their schools.

Blackburn with Darwen Borough Council

Joanne Siddle, Deputy Director Education and Schools at BwD Borough Council, for her partnership and ceaselessly helping me share my content to support SLT, teaching staff and their pupils.

My good friend Maureen Bateson MBE, Andrea Sturgess, Sayyed Osman MBE and staff, for always supporting me and their partnership, which has helped countless children in hard times.

I will finish by leaving you all one of my very own quotes that I live by.

THEY WILL NEVER KNOW THE DIFFERENCE
THEY MAKE TO US,
AS WE MAKE A DIFFERENCE TO THEM.
JOHN MAGEE